Why Would a Good God Allow Suffering?

DISCOVERY SERIES BIBLE STUDY
For individuals or groups

T'S AN OLD QUESTION. Four thousand years ago, a victim of personal, family, and financial reversals spoke to the silent heavens and pleaded, "Show me why You contend with me. Does it seem good to You that You should oppress, that You should despise the work of Your hands?" (. . .) The questions are still being asked. "Does God ! . . . . why He is all . . wing me to suffer like this? Wł . . . . .

There are answers. . . . . keep our pain in perspective. I . . . . uffering to work for us. In the following pages, ... ı, who for many years was managing editor of *Our Daily Bread,* shows us that while heaven may not be answering all our questions, it is giving us all the answers we need to trust and love the One who, in our pain, is calling us to himself.

—*Bill Crowder*
Associate Teacher, RBC Ministries

This Discovery Series Bible Study is based on
Why Would A Good God Allow Suffering? (Q0106), one of the popular Discovery Series
booklets from RBC Ministries. Find out more about Discovery Series at
www.discoveryseries.org

Managing Editor: Dave Branon
Study Guide questions: Sim Kay Tee, Dave Branon
Graphic Design: Steve Gier
Cover Photo: Attilio Lombardo / stock.xchg

ISBN: 978-157293-553-2
Printed in the United States of America

First printing in 2011

Table of Contents

How To Use
DISCOVERY SERIES BIBLE STUDIES

The Purpose

The Discovery Series Bible Study (DSBS) series provides assistance to pastors and lay leaders in guiding and teaching fellow Christians with lessons adapted from RBC Ministries Discovery Series booklets and supplemented from items taken from the pages of *Our Daily Bread*. The DSBS series uses the inductive study method to help Christians understand the Bible more clearly.

The Format

READ: Each DSBS book is divided into a series of lessons. For each lesson, you will read a few pages that will give you insight into one aspect of the overall study. Included in some studies will be FOCAL POINT and TIME OUT FOR THEOLOGY segments to help you think through the material. These can be used as discussion starters for group sessions.

RESPOND: At the end of the reading is a two-page STUDY GUIDE to help participants respond to and reflect on the subject. If you are the leader of a group study, ask each member to preview the STUDY GUIDE before the group gets together. Don't feel that you have to work your way through each question in the STUDY GUIDE; let the interest level of the participants dictate the flow of the discussion. The questions are designed for either group or individual study. Here are the parts of that guide:

MEMORY VERSE: A short Scripture passage that focuses your thinking on the biblical truth at hand and can be used for memorization. You might suggest memorization as a part of each meeting.

WARMING UP: A general interest question that can foster discussion (group) or contemplation (individual).

THINKING THROUGH: Questions that will help a group or a student interact with the reading. These questions help drive home the critical concepts of the book.

DIGGING IN: An inductive study of a related passage of Scripture, reminding the group or the student of the importance of Scripture as the final authority.

GOING FURTHER: A two-part wrap-up of the response: REFER suggests ways to compare the ideas of the lesson with teachings in other parts of the Bible. REFLECT challenges the group or the learner to apply the teaching in real life.

OUR DAILY BREAD: After each STUDY GUIDE sessions will be an *Our Daily Bread* article that relates to the topic. You can use this for further reflection or for an introduction to a time of prayer.

Go to the Leader's and User's Guide on page 56 for further suggestions about using the Discovery Series Bible Study.

1

Elusive Answers

Life can be hard to understand. In trying to come to grips with the cold realities of our existence, we can easily become frustrated. We long for answers to the immense problem of suffering. We may even wonder if we will ever fully comprehend why bad things happen to good people and why good things happen to bad people. The answers often seem to be elusive, hidden, out-of-reach.

Oh, it makes sense that a terrorist would be killed by his own bomb. It makes sense that a reckless driver would be in a serious accident. It makes sense that a person who plays with fire would get burned. It even makes sense that a chain-smoker would develop lung cancer.

But what about the innocent men, women, and children who are killed by a terrorist's bomb? What about the young driver who suffers severe brain damage because a drunk veered over the center line? What about the person whose home burns down due to no fault of his own? And what about the 2-year-old child with leukemia?

It is dangerous, even foolish, to pretend that we have a complete answer as to why God allows suffering.

The reasons are many and complex. It's just as wrong to demand that we should understand. When the Old Testament sufferer Job realized that he had no right to demand an answer from God, he said, "Therefore I have uttered what I did not understand, things too wonderful for me, which I did not know" (Job 42:3).

 ## Some Answers

But God has given us some answers. Although we may not be able to know why one person gets singled out for a disease, we can know part of the reason why diseases exist. And even though we may not understand why we face a certain problem, we can know how to deal with the situation and respond in a way that pleases the Lord.

One more thing. I am not going to pretend that I fully understand the suffering that you personally may be experiencing. Although some aspects of human pain are common, the particulars are different. And what you may need most right now is not a four-point outline on why you are suffering or even what to do about it. What you may need most is a hug, a listening ear, or someone who will just sit with you in silence. Sometime along the way, however, you will want and need the truths of God's Word to comfort you and help you to see your plight from God's perspective.

You and I need more than untested theories. That's why in the pages that follow I have tried to include the insights of people who have suffered a variety of physical and emotional pains. My prayer for you is that your faith in God will stand firm even when your world seems to be falling apart.

Where Is God?

In our world of pain, where is God? If He is good and compassionate, why is life often so tragic? Has He lost control? Or, if He is in control, what is He trying to do to me and to others?

Some people have chosen to deny God's existence because they cannot imagine a God who would allow such misery. Some believe that God exists, but they want nothing to do with Him because they don't think He could be good. Others have settled for a belief in a kindly God who loves us but has lost control of a rebellious planet. Still others cling tenaciously to a belief in an all-wise, all-powerful, loving God who somehow uses evil for good.

As we search the Bible, we discover that it paints a picture of a God who can do anything He chooses to do. Sometimes He has acted in mercy and performed miracles in behalf of His people. At other times, though, He has chosen to do nothing to stop tragedy. He is supposed to be intimately involved in our lives, yet at times He seems deaf to our cries for help. In the Bible, He assures us that He controls all that happens, but He sometimes lets us be the targets of evil people, bad genes, dangerous viruses, or natural disasters.

If you're like me, you long for some way to put together an answer to this puzzling issue of suffering. I believe that God has given us enough pieces of the puzzle to help us trust Him even when we don't have all the information we would like. In this brief study we will see that the basic answers of the Bible are that our good God allows pain and suffering in our world to alert us to the problem of sin, to direct us to respond to Him in faith and hope, to shape us to be more like Christ, and to unite us so that we will help each other.

Elusive Answers

To recognize the problem of suffering and the challenge of seeing God's role in that suffering.

MEMORY VERSE
Job 42:1,2—

"I know that You can do everything, and that no purpose of Yours can be withheld from You."

Warming Up

Identify a recent experience—sickness, failure, disappointment, betrayal, trial, suffering—that caused you to wonder if God had been unfair to you. How have you dealt with your questions? What answers have you found?

Thinking Through

1. Respond to the John Stott quote on page 7. Do you agree? What Scriptures would you use to challenge or to support such an idea?

2. On pages 8–9, Kurt offers some different views of the character and nature of God. Do you believe God is all-powerful? All-good? Both? Neither? On what do you base your view?

3. The issue of suffering and the character of God is compared to a puzzle (see p. 9). What makes it a puzzling issue to you?

Going Further

Refer

Compare the experiences of Job to those of Joseph (Genesis 37–50). In what ways are they similar? In what ways are they different?

1. What are the events in Job's life (Job 1:13–2:13) that shaped his questioning and complaints?

2. According to the biblical context of 42:3, what was Job's response to the life-experiences he endured? What was Job's ultimate response (vv.1–6), and why was it a tough admission to make?

3. In verse 3, Job was left to conclude that if God had the power and wisdom to create this world (Job 38–41), there is reason to trust Him in times of suffering. Why is trusting God during a hardship a reasonable response to His creation?

[1] Then Job answered the Lord and said: 2 "I know that You can do everything, and that no purpose of Yours can be withheld from You. 3 You asked, 'Who is this who hides counsel without knowledge?' Therefore I have uttered what I did not understand, things are too wonderful for me, which I did not know. 4 Listen, please, and let me speak; You said, 'I will question you, and you shall answer Me.' 5 "I have heard of You by the hearing of my ear, but now my eye sees You. 6 Therefore I abhor myself, and repent in dust and ashes."

Prayer Time

Use the *Our Daily Bread* article on the next page as a guide for a devotional and meditation time relating to suffering.

Reflect

1. Think about past tragedies you have witnessed or experienced. What was your response to those events?

2. Paul wrote, "We walk by faith, not by sight" (2 Corinthians 5:7). How can you apply this verse to the suffering you see in life?

An Age-old Question

Seventeen-year-old Jeremy was struggling with a question theologians have wrestled with for centuries. But for him the problem was not academic; it was real. He was trying to understand why his mother had to have brain surgery. He asked, "Why do good people suffer, Mom?"

She told him, "Suffering is part of living in a sin-cursed world, and good people suffer like anybody else. That's why I'm glad we have Jesus. If I die, I'll go to a better place, and I'll long for the day when I can see you again." She then said that she could understand his frustration, but she told him not to put the blame on God.

If you and I are baffled by the suffering of good people, we can put the question squarely before God, argue with Him if we must, and struggle with our doubts. But let's not blame Him.

God didn't explain to Job what He was doing but said that He could be trusted to do what is right (Job 38–42). And He has assured us in His Word that Jesus suffered on our behalf, rose from the dead, and is preparing a suffering-free place for us.

These may not be the answers we want, but they are the answers we need to help us live with that age-old and often unanswerable question of suffering.

—*Dennis De Haan*

JOB
2:10—

In all this Job did not sin with his lips.

■ Read today's
Our Daily Bread at
www.rbc.org/odb

Suffering:
To Alert Us

PART 1

Imagine a world without pain. What would it be like? At first the idea may sound appealing. No more headaches. No more backaches. No more upset stomachs. No more throbbing sensations when the hammer misses the mark and lands on your thumb. No more sore throats. But there would also be no more sensation to alert you of a broken bone or tearing ligaments. No alarm to let you know that an ulcer is eating a hole in your stomach. No discomfort to warn of a cancerous tumor that is gathering forces for a takeover of your body. No angina to let you know that the blood vessels to your heart are clogging up. No pain to signal a ruptured appendix.

As much as we may abhor pain, we have to admit that it often serves a good purpose. It warns us when something goes wrong. The cause of the misery, rather than the agony itself, is the real problem. Pain is merely a symptom, a siren or bell that sounds when a part of the body is endangered or under attack. In sessions two and three we will see how pain could be God's way to alert us that: 1. Something's wrong with the world. 2. Something's wrong with God's creatures. 3. Something's wrong with me.

Any one of these problems could be the reason for the pain in our lives. Let's look at each possible diagnosis in this session and the next.

 # Something's Wrong With the World

The sorry condition of our planet indicates that something has gone terribly wrong. The suffering we experience and the distress we sense in others indicate that suffering does not discriminate on the basis of race, social status, religion, or even morality. It can seem cruel, random, purposeless, grotesque, and wildly out of control. Bad things happen to people who try to be good, and good things happen to people who enjoy being bad.

The seeming unfairness of it all has struck close to each of us. I remember watching my grandmother as she was dying of cancer. Grandma and Grandpa Blohm moved in with our family. My mother, a registered nurse, took care of her during her final months. Mom administered the pain killer. Grandpa desperately wanted her to be healed. Then the day came when the hearse pulled up and took away her frail, wasted body. I knew she was in heaven, but it still hurt. I hated cancer—I still do.

As I sit here thinking of all the suffering that my friends, co-workers, family, neighbors, and church family have experienced, I can hardly believe the length of the list—and my list is incomplete. So often these people have suffered through no apparent fault of their own. An accident, a birth defect, a genetic disorder, a miscarriage, an abusive parent, chronic pain, a rebellious child, a severe illness, random disease, the death of a spouse or a child, a broken relationship, a natural disaster. It just doesn't seem fair. From time to time I'm tempted to give in to frustration.

How do we resolve this? How do we live with the cold facts of life without denying reality or being overcome with despair? Couldn't God have created a world where nothing would ever go wrong? Couldn't He have made a world where people would never have the ability to make a bad choice or ever hurt another person? Couldn't He have made a world where mosquitoes, weeds, and cancer would never exist? He could have—but He didn't.

The great gift of human freedom that He has given to us, the ability to choose, carries with it the risk of making wrong choices. If you could choose between being a free-thinking creature in a world where bad choices produce suffering, or being a robot in a world without pain, what would you decide? What kind of being would bring more honor to God? What kind of creature would love Him more?

We could have been created to be like the cute battery-operated dolls that say "I love you" when hugged. But God had other plans. He took a "risk" to create beings who could do the unthinkable—rebel against their Creator.

■ FOCAL POINT

Broken homes, broken hearts, broken bodies broken hopes, broken health. Broken vows, broken lives—what sadness in those words! But this is merely the course of nature. Broken things suggest accidents and calamaties. We associate them with disappointments and failure. But all these "tragedies" are known to God, and He can bring out of those broken fragments something far better, more beautiful, more enduring than that precious thing which was broken at our feet.

—Dr. M. R. De Haan
Broken Things

What happened in paradise? Temptation, bad choices, and tragic consequences destroyed the tranquility of Adam and Eve's existence. Genesis 2 and 3 detail how Satan tested their love for the Lord—and they failed. In biblical terms, that failure is called sin. And just as the AIDS virus infects a body, breaks down the body's immune system, and can lead to death, so also sin spreads as a deadly infection that passes from one generation to the next. Each new generation inherits the effects of sin and the desire to sin (Romans 1:18–32; 5:12, 15, 18).

Not only did the entrance of sin into the world have devastating effects on the nature of human beings, but sin also brought about immediate and continual judgment from God. Genesis 3 relates how physical and spiritual

■ FOCAL POINT

"For the earnest expectation of the creation eagerly waits for the revealing of the sons of God. For the creation was subjected to futility, not willingly, but because of Him who subjected it in hope; because the creation itself also will be delivered from the bondage of corruption into the glorious liberty of the children of God. For we know that the whole creation groans and labors with birth pangs together until now."

—Romans 8:19–22

death became a part of human existence (vv. 3, 19), childbirth became painful (v. 16), the ground was cursed with weeds that would make man's work very difficult (vv. 17–19), and Adam and Eve were evicted from the special Garden where they had enjoyed intimate fellowship with God (vv. 23–24).

In the New Testament, the apostle Paul described the whole creation of God as groaning and eagerly anticipating the time when it will be freed from the curse of decay and be remade—free from the effects of sin (Romans 8:19–22).

Disease, disaster, and corruption are symptoms of a deeper problem—the human race has rebelled against the Creator. Every sorrow, grief, and agony is a vivid reminder of our human predicament. Like a huge neon sign, the reality of suffering screams the message that the world is not the way God created it to be.

Therefore, the first and most basic answer to the problem of the existence of suffering is that it is the direct result of sin's entrance into the world. Pain alerts us that a spiritual disease is wracking our planet. Many times our troubles may be merely the side-effects of living in a fallen world, through no direct fault of our own.

2 Suffering: To Alert Us (Part 1)

STUDY GUIDE

read pages 13–17

To understand a positive contribution of pain and suffering to us as it warns us of danger.

MEMORY VERSE
2 Peter 3:9—
"The Lord is not slack concerning His promise, ... but is longsuffering toward us, not willing that any should perish but that all should come to repentance."

Warming Up

Imagine a world without pain. What would it be like? In what ways is pain a blessing? In what ways is it a curse?

Thinking Through

1. On page 15, we are told that God "took a risk" in choosing to create us in the way He did. What was that risk, and how real was it?

2. Explain how sin, which first occured in the Garden of Eden, has infected all of mankind.

3. One of the main concepts being explained in this section is that the problems of this world are self-inflicted by mankind. How does Romans 8:19–22 help us see that the world we live in is not a perfect world?

Going Further

Refer

Jesus said that suffering is not always a direct result of sin (see Luke 13:2–5, John 9:1–3). What are some other possible explanations for human suffering? (See Exodus 4:11; Job 1:8–12, 2:3–6; John 9:3; 11:4.)

1. What has gone "terribly wrong" wrong with the world, according to Romans 1:18?

2. Some people say there is no evidence that God exists. What does Romans 1:19–20 say about that idea?

> 18 For the wrath of God is revealed from heaven against all ungodliness and unrighteousness of men, who suppress the truth in unrighteousness, 19 because what may be known of God is manifest in them, for God has shown it to them. 20 For since the creation of the world His invisible attributes are clearly seen, being understood by the things that are made, even His eternal power and Godhead, so that they are without excuse, 21 because, although they knew God, they did not glorify Him as God, nor were thankful, but became futile in their thoughts, and their foolish hearts were darkened.

3. Verse 21 seems to indicate that people who can't find it in their hearts to be grateful to God create their own problems. Describe what Paul says those problems might look like.

Prayer Time ➤

Use the *Our Daily Bread* article on the next page as a guide for a devotional and meditation time relating to suffering.

Reflect

It appears that Christians and non-Christians alike have a responsibility to see God in their circumstances. When have you responded more like a non-believer than a believer when trouble has visited your life? Can you see that God might have been trying to get your attention?

Invisible Gold

In the 1980s, Northern Nevada was the site of a gold strike. The discovery would have been beyond the imagination of 19th-century prospectors, for the gold in those western hills is virtually invisible. Even after being magnified 1,500 times, most of the particles remain imperceptible.

Modern technology, however, has found a way to extract the gold. First, tons of ore are crushed to the consistency of fine sand. Then cyanide is added to dissolve the granules into a clear solution. When zinc dust is blended in, the gold separates from the mixture. The gold was there all the time, but it couldn't be seen.

There's a similarity here to Peter's explanation of suffering in his first New Testament letter. He saw great potential in the mountains of adversity and affliction that faced the Lord's people. So he encouraged them to look beyond the heat and pressure produced by their suffering to the precious faith the Lord was developing from it (1 Peter 1:6–7). He showed them that the "faith processing" experience was of great value to their spiritual lives. Therefore, they could actually rejoice in it (v. 8).

Don't give in to life's troubles. You may not see in them the rich potential of a strong faith, but it's there. To have it developed is much more precious than gold!

—*Mart De Haan*

1 PETER 1:6–7—

The genuineness of your faith, being much more precious than gold that perishes, though it is tested by fire, may be found to praise, honor, and glory at the revelation of Jesus Christ, whom having not seen you love.

■ Read today's *Our Daily Bread* at **www.rbc.org/odb**

3

Suffering: To Alert Us

PART 2

Something's Wrong With God's Creatures

We can be targets of cruel acts from other people or from Satan's rebel army. Both fallen human beings and fallen spirit beings (angels who have rebelled) have the capacity to make decisions that damage themselves and others.

SUFFERING CAN BE CAUSED BY PEOPLE

As free (and sin-infected) creatures, people have made and will continue to make many bad choices in life. These bad choices often affect other people.

For example, one of Adam's sons, Cain, made a choice to kill his brother

Abel (Genesis 4:7–8). Lamech boasted about his violence (vv. 23–24). Sarai mistreated Hagar (16:1–6). Laban swindled his nephew Jacob (29:15–30). Joseph's brothers sold him into slavery (37:12–36), and then Potiphar's wife falsely accused him of attempted rape and had him thrown into prison (39). Pharaoh cruelly mistreated the Jewish slaves in Egypt (Exodus 1). King Herod slaughtered all the babies who lived in and around Bethlehem in an attempt to kill Jesus (Matthew 2:16–18).

The hurt that others inflict on us may be due to selfishness on their part. Or we may be the target of persecution because of our faith in Christ. Throughout history, people who have identified with the Lord have suffered at the hands of those who rebelled against God.

Before his conversion, Saul was a rabid anti-Christian who did all he could to make life miserable for believers—even working to have them put to death (Acts 7:54–8:3). But after his dramatic turn to the Lord Jesus, he bravely endured all types of persecution as he boldly proclaimed the gospel message (2 Corinthians 4:7–12; 6:1–10). He could even say that the suffering he endured helped to make him more like Christ (Philippians 3:10).

SUFFERING CAN ALSO BE CAUSED BY SATAN AND DEMONS

Job's life story is a vivid example of how a good person can suffer incredible tragedy because of satanic attack. God allowed Satan to take away Job's possessions, his family, and his health (Job 1–2).

I cringed even as I wrote the preceding sentence. Somehow, and for His own reasons, God allowed Satan to devastate Job's life. We may tend to compare this to a father who allows the neighborhood bully to beat up his children just to see if they would still love Dad afterward. But, as Job came to realize, that's not a fair assessment when speaking about our wise and loving God.

We know, though Job did not, that his life was a test case, a living testimonial to the trustworthiness of God. Job illustrated that a person can trust God and maintain integrity even when life falls apart (for whatever reason), because God is worth trusting. In the end, Job learned that even though he didn't understand what God was up to, he had plenty of reason to believe that God was not being unjust, cruel, sadistic, or unfair by allowing his life to be ripped apart (Job 42).

The apostle Paul experienced a physical problem that he attributed to Satan. He called it a "thorn in the flesh . . . , a messenger of Satan to buffet me" (2 Corinthians 12:7). Paul prayed to be freed from the problem, but God didn't give him what he asked for. Instead, the Lord helped him to see how this difficulty could serve a good purpose. It made Paul humbly dependent on the Lord and put him in a position to experience His grace (vv. 8–10).

Although most cases of sickness cannot be directly tied to Satan's work, the Gospel accounts do record a few examples of suffering attributed to Satan, including a blind and mute man (Matthew 12:22) and a boy who suffered seizures (17:14–18).

 # Something's Wrong With Me

Too often when something goes wrong in our lives we immediately jump to the conclusion that God is whipping us because of some sin we've committed. That's not necessarily true. As I indicated in the previous points, much of the suffering that comes into our lives is because we live in a broken world inhabited by broken people and rebellious spirit beings.

Job's friends mistakenly thought that he was suffering because of sin in his life (Job 4:7–8; 8:1–6; 22:4–5; 36:17). Jesus' own disciples jumped to the wrong conclusion when they saw a blind man. They wondered if the man's sight problem was due to his personal sin or because of something his parents had done (John 9:1–2). Jesus told them that the man's physical problem was not related to his personal sin or the sin of his parents (v. 3).

With these cautions in mind, we need to deal with the hard truth that some suffering does come as the direct consequence of sin—either as corrective discipline from God for those He loves, or punitive action by God upon rebels in His universe.

CORRECTION

If you and I have placed our trust in Jesus Christ as our Savior, we are children of God. As such, we are part of a family headed by a loving Father who trains and corrects us. He's not an abusive, sadistic parent who dishes out severe beatings because He gets some twisted pleasure out of it. Hebrews 12:5–6 and 9–10 spell out the real reason for godly correction.

And to the church in Laodicea, Jesus said, "As many as I love, I rebuke and chasten. Therefore be zealous and repent" (Revelation 3:19).

King David knew what it was like to experience the tough love of the Lord. After his adultery with Bathsheba and his conniving to ensure that her husband would be killed in battle, David did not repent until the prophet Nathan confronted him. Psalm 51 recounts David's struggle with guilt and his cry for forgiveness. In another psalm, David reflected on the effects of covering up and ignoring sin. He wrote, "When I kept silent, my bones grew old through my groaning all the day long. For day and night Your hand was heavy upon me" (Psalm 32:3–4).

In 1 Corinthians 11:27–32, the apostle Paul warned believers that treating the things of the Lord lightly—partaking of the Lord's Supper without taking it seriously—will bring discipline. Paul explained that this discipline of the Lord was purposeful. He said, "But when we are judged, we are chastened by the Lord, that we may not be condemned with the world" (v. 32).

Most of us can understand the principle that whom God loves He disciplines. We would expect a loving Father to correct us and call us to renew our obedience to Him.

JUDGMENT

God also acts to deal with stubborn unbelievers who persist in doing evil. A person who has not received God's gift of salvation can expect to receive God's wrath at a future day of judgment and faces the danger of harsh judgment now if God so chooses.

The Lord brought the flood to destroy decadent humanity (Genesis 6). He destroyed Sodom and Gomorrah (Genesis 18–19). He sent plagues on the Egyptians (Exodus 7–12). He commanded Israel to completely destroy the pagans who inhabited the Promised Land (Deuteronomy 7:1–3). He struck down the arrogant King Herod of New Testament times (Acts 12:19–23). And at the future day of judgment, God will deal out perfect justice to all those who reject His love and rule (2 Peter 2:4–9).

In the here-and-now, however, we face inequities. For His all-wise reasons, God has chosen to delay His perfect justice. The psalm writer Asaph struggled with this apparent unfairness of life. He wrote about the wicked who were getting away with their evil deeds, even prospering, while many of the righteous were having troubles (Psalm 73). Concerning the prosperity of the wicked he said, "When I thought how to understand this, it was too painful for me—until I went into the sanctuary of God; then I understood their end" (vv. 16–17). By thinking of and worshiping the sovereign Lord of the universe, Asaph was able to get things back into perspective.

When we struggle with the reality that wicked people are literally "getting away with murder" and all sorts of immorality, we need to remember that "the Lord is . . . longsuffering toward us, not willing that any should perish but that all should come to repentence" (2 Peter 3:9).

The first part of the answer, then, to the problem of suffering is that God uses it to alert us to serious problems. Pain sounds the alarm that indicates something is wrong with the world, with humanity at large, and with you and me. But as we will see in the next section, God not only signals the problems, but He also uses troubles to encourage us to find the solutions—in Him.

3 Suffering: To Alert Us (Part 2)

STUDY GUIDE

read pages 21–25

To be reminded that trouble is often the result of fallen people (including us) acting fallen.

MEMORY VERSE

Job 2:10 —
"Shall we indeed accept good from God, and shall we not accept adversity?"

Warming Up

Can you think of a time when something bad happened to someone and you felt you knew the reason why? When you think about it, how easy is it generally to know the "why" in these situations?

Thinking Through

1. How can we tell the difference between hurt others inflict on us due to selfishness and problems caused by persecution (p. 22)? Have you ever wondered which was which in your life?

2. Few things have such a far-reaching impact as the choices we make. One example is David's experience discussed on page 24. How can your choices produce suffering for you? For others in your life?

3. How often have you felt as Asaph felt in Psalm 73—wishing God would not let unbelievers be so successful? Where did Asaph go to get the help he needed?

Going Further

Refer

Examine these verses to learn what they tell us about God's discipline: Hebrews 12:5, 11; Proverbs 12:11; Revelation 3:19.

1. How does the text in Hebrews 12 distinguish between loving correction and brutal abuse? What does discipline demonstrate about your relationship with God? How does His discipline differ from human discipline?

2. Compare the verbs the writer of Hebrews used to describe correction—*chastening, rebuked, scourges.* What would have been the connotation of those terms in the culture of the first century? What are the applications of those terms in today's world?

3. Revelation 3:19, Psalm 32:3–4, and 1 Corinthians 11:27–32 are used on pages 24 to reinforce the assertion of Hebrews 12 that discipline and correction are acts of love. Compare and contrast the circumstances of discipline described in each passage.

⁵ And you have forgotten the exhortation which speaks to you as to sons:
"My son, do not despise the chastening of the LORD,
Nor be discouraged when you are rebuked by Him;
⁶ For whom the LORD loves He chastens,
And scourges every son whom He receives."
⁹ Furthermore, we have had human fathers who corrected us, and we paid them respect. Shall we not much more readily be in subjection to the Father of spirits and live? ¹⁰ For they indeed for a few days chastened us as seemed best to them, but He for our profit, that we may be partakers of His holiness.

Prayer Time ▷

Use the *Our Daily Bread* article on the next page as a guide for a devotional and meditation time relating to suffering.

Reflect

1. When have you felt God's corrective hand on your life? How did that turn out?

2. How has God's chastening helped you develop the holiness mentioned in Hebrews 12:10?

Tough or Easy?

The Christian life—is it tough or easy? Which is it supposed to be? Does our faith in Jesus Christ cause us difficulty, hardship, suffering, and loss? Or does it pave for us an easy road to heaven?

These aren't easy questions. But if we look at some of the people in the Bible—the ones we admire and respect for their obvious faithfulness to the Lord—we see that they didn't have a life of ease. Paul, for example, faced difficulties that would make most of us wonder where God is: shipwrecks, imprisonments, beatings, and other kinds of abuse (2 Corinthians 11:23–28). It seems he was better off before he started following Jesus.

In his book *Amusing Ourselves To Death,* social critic Neil Postman wrote, "Christianity is a serious and demanding religion. When it is delivered as easy and amusing, it is another kind of religion altogether." He's right. Jesus himself said, "If anyone desires to come after Me, let him deny himself, and take up his cross, and follow Me" (Matthew 16:24). That's a clear call for self-denial.

Paul was given a task, and he did it wholeheartedly for God's glory, no matter what the cost (Acts 20:24). Are we willing to do what God has called us to do with the same dedication, whether it is easy or tough?

—*Dave Branon*

ACTS 20:24—

But none of these things move me; nor do I count my life dear to myself, so that I may finish my race with joy.

■ Read today's *Our Daily Bread* at **www.rbc.org/odb**

4

Suffering:
To Direct Us

When a person turns away from God, suffering often gets the blame. But strangely, suffering also gets the credit when people describe what redirected their lives, helped them to see life more clearly, and caused their relationship with God to grow closer. How can similar circumstances have such radically different effects on people? The reasons lie deep within the people, not the events.

A well-known and outspoken media leader publicly denounced Christianity as "a religion for losers." But he has not always felt that way. As a young man he had Bible training, including a Christian prep school. When joking about the heavy indoctrination he received, he said, "I think I was saved seven or eight times." But then a painful experience changed his outlook on life and God. His younger sister became very ill. He prayed for her healing, but after five years of suffering she died. He became disillusioned with a God who would allow that to happen. He said, "I began to lose my faith, and the more I lost it the better I felt."

Joni's Story

What makes the difference between someone like him and a person like Joni Eareckson Tada? In *Where Is God When It Hurts?* Philip Yancey describes the gradual transformation that took place in Joni's attitude in the years after she was paralyzed in a diving accident.

"At first, Joni found it impossible to reconcile her condition with her belief in a loving God. . . . The turning to God was very gradual. A melting in her attitude from bitterness to trust dragged out over three years of tears and violent questioning" (pp. 133–134).

A turning point came the evening that a close friend, Cindy, told her, "Joni, you aren't the only one. Jesus knows how you feel—why, He was paralyzed too." Cindy described how Jesus was fastened to the cross, paralyzed by the nails.

> ■ **FOCAL POINT**
>
> "My grace is sufficient for you, for My strength is made perfect in weakness."
> —2 Corinthians 12:9

Yancey then observed, "The thought intrigued Joni and, for a moment, took her mind off her own pain. It had never occurred to her that God might have felt the same piercing sensations that now racked her body. The realization was profoundly comforting" (p. 134).

Instead of continuing to search for why the devastating accident occurred, Joni has been forced to depend more heavily on the Lord and to look at life from a long-range perspective.

Yancey further says about Joni, "She wrestled with God, yes, but she did not turn away from Him. . . . Joni now calls her accident a 'glorious intruder,' and claims it was the best thing that ever happened to her. God used it to get her attention and direct her thoughts toward Him" (pp. 137–138).

This principle that suffering can produce healthy dependence on God is taught by the apostle Paul in one of his letters to the church in Corinth. He wrote:

We do not want you to be ignorant, brethren, of our trouble which came to us in Asia: that we were burdened beyond measure, above strength, so that we despaired even of life. Yes, we had the sentence of death in ourselves, that we should not trust in ourselves but in God who raises the dead (2 Corinthians 1:8–9).

Paul's Comments

A similar idea can be found in Paul's comments about his physical troubles. The Lord told Paul, "My grace is sufficient for you, for My strength is made perfect in weakness" (2 Corinthians 12:9). Then Paul added, "Therefore I take pleasure in infirmities, in reproaches, in needs, in persecutions, in distresses, for Christ's sake. For when I am weak, then I am strong" (v. 10).

Suffering has a way of showing how weak our own resources really are. It forces us to rethink priorities, values, goals, dreams, pleasures, the source of real strength, and our relationships with people and with God. It has a way of directing our attention to spiritual realities—if we don't turn from God instead.

Suffering forces us to evaluate the direction of our lives. We can choose to despair by focusing on our present problems, or we can choose to hope by recognizing God's long-range plan for us (Romans 5:5; 8:18–28; Hebrews 11).

Of all the passages in the Bible, Hebrews 11 most reassures me that whether life is grand or grotesque, my response needs to be one of faith in the wisdom, power, and control of God. No matter what, I have good reason to trust Him—just as the great men and women of old hoped in Him.

For example, Hebrews 11 reminds us about Noah, a man who spent 120 years waiting for God to fulfill His promise of a devastating flood (Genesis 6:3).

Abraham waited many agonizing years before the child whom God had promised was finally born. Joseph was sold into slavery and wrongfully imprisoned, but he finally saw how God used all the apparent evil in his life for a good purpose (Genesis 50:20). Moses waited until he was 80 years old before God used him to help deliver the Jews from Egypt. And even then, leading those faith-deficient people was a struggle (see Exodus).

Hebrews 11 lists people like Gideon, Samson, David, and Samuel, who saw great victories as they lived for the Lord. But in the middle of verse 35 the mood changes. Suddenly we are face-to-face with people who had to endure incredible suffering—people who died without seeing why God allowed them to undergo such tragedies. These individuals were tortured, jeered, flogged, stoned, cut in half, stabbed, mistreated, and forced to live as outcasts (vv. 35–38). God had planned that only in the long-range view of eternity would their faithfulness during hardship be rewarded (vv. 39–40).

Pain forces us to look beyond our immediate circumstances. Suffering drives us to ask the big questions of "Why am I here?" and "What's the purpose of my life?" By pursuing those questions and finding the answers in the God of the Bible, we will find the stability we need to endure even the worst that life can inflict because we know that this present life is not all there is. When we understand that a sovereign God is standing over all of human history and weaving it all together in a beautiful tapestry that will ultimately glorify Him, then we can see things in better perspective.

In Romans 8:18 the apostle Paul wrote, "For I consider that the sufferings of this present time are not worthy to be compared with the glory which shall be revealed in us." Paul was not making light of our troubles, but he was telling believers to see our present troubles in light of all eternity. Our problems may indeed be heavy, even crushing. But Paul said that when compared to the incredible glories that await those who love God, even the darkest and most burdensome circumstances of life will fade by comparison.

We need to take time to look at one more example, perhaps the most significant illustration we could consider. The day that Christ hung on the cross is now referred to as Good Friday. At the time, it was anything but a good day. It was a day of intense suffering, anguish, darkness, and gloom. It was a day when Jesus felt all alone. It was a day when God seemed absent and silent, when evil seemed to triumph, and hopes were dashed. But then came Sunday. Jesus rose from the grave. That awesome event put Friday in a different light. The resurrection gave a whole new meaning to what happened on the cross. Instead of being a time of defeat, it became a day of triumph.

We too can look ahead. We can endure our dark "Fridays" and be able to look on them as "good" because we serve the God of Sunday.

So when troubles strike, and they will, remember this: God uses such situations to direct us to Him and to the long-range view of life. He calls for us to trust, to hope, to wait.

Suffering: To Direct Us

STUDY GUIDE
read pages 29–33

4

To understand the ways that suffering can draw us to God.

MEMORY VERSE
Romans 8:18—
"I consider that the sufferings of this present time are not worthy to be compared with the glory which shall be revealed in us."

Warming Up

The idea that suffering can either drive us from God or to Him is a sobering thought. Examples of both responses are given on pages 29–30. Can you think of any other examples? Can you give examples from your own life?

Thinking Through

1. Why do you think it was comforting to Joni (p. 30) when she discovered that God understood completely the pain she suffered and that Jesus had suffered that pain himself?

2. Consider the change of heart that allowed Joni to view the paralyzing accident as a "glorious intruder" (p. 30). How does this model the redirecting of her heart away from bitterness and to faith and hope in God? If not a "glorious intruder," what two words would you use to describe your suffering?

3. It is impossible to think very long about the issue of suffering without turning to the cross and seeing the suffering of Christ. How does that suffering, and its ultimate vindication in the resurrection, illustrate Paul's wonderful declaration in Romans 8:18? How do you respond to that declaration?

Going Further

Refer

As you look with hope for God's ultimate response to pain and suffering in the world, it is helpful to consider "the rest of the story." Look at Revelation 21:1–5 and describe how it relates to Paul's words in Romans 8:18.

1. In the context of 2 Corinthians 12, we are confronted with Paul's suffering for the gospel in chapter 11. How does this suffering differ from his "thorn in the flesh" in 2 Corinthians 12:7? _____

_____

_____

_____

_____

2. In verse 8, Paul described his prayers for deliverance—prayers that were answered in the negative. What is it about grace that makes it a better answer to Paul's prayer than healing would have been?

_____

_____

_____

_____

_____

_____

[7] Lest I should be exalted above measure by the abundance of the revelations, a thorn in the flesh was given to me, a messenger of Satan to buffet me, lest I be exalted above measure. [8] Concerning this thing I pleaded with the Lord three times that it might depart from me. [9] And He said to me, "My grace is sufficient for you, for My strength is made perfect in weakness." [10] Therefore most gladly I will rather boast in my infirmities, that the power of Christ may rest upon me. Therefore I take pleasure in infirmities, in reproaches, in needs, in persecutions, in distresses, for Christ's sake. For when I am weak, then I am strong.

3. What is it that enabled Paul to say that he took "pleasure in infirmities, in reproaches, in needs, in persecutions, in distresses" (v. 10)? _____

_____

_____

_____

_____

Prayer Time ▶

Use the *Our Daily Bread* article on the next page as a guide for a devotional and meditation time relating to suffering.

Reflect

Do you live with an outlook of hope or an outlook of despair? What steps of personal growth are you willing to experience to see that hope formed in you? _____

_____

_____

_____

Shared Tears

Suffering can become so intense at times that we don't know how we can take any more pain. It's in these moments that Jesus reassures us of His presence and sustains us, even though for reasons we do not understand the hurt is not taken away.

Dr. Diane Komp, a pediatric cancer specialist at Yale University, often must perform very painful procedures on children. She tells of a wonderful nurse's aide named JoAnn who reflects God's love. During the procedures, JoAnn comes in and holds the child and tells him that she will stay with him. Her hugs, along with her loving and reassuring words, have carried many children through those difficult times.

That's a glimpse of what Jesus does for those who trust Him in their suffering. He draws us to himself and says that He will be with us in our pain, for nothing can separate us from His love (Romans 8:39).

How often we cry out for release, but no relief comes. The pain persists, but we sense God's presence. Later, as we look back, we can see how the Lord was with us, caring for us, meeting our deepest needs.

No matter what painful situation you may face today, remember that Jesus is holding you.

—Dennis De Haan

ROMANS 8:39—

No height nor depth, nor any other created thing, shall be able to separate us from the love of God which is in Christ Jesus our Lord.

■ Read today's
Our Daily Bread at
www.rbc.org/odb

5

Suffering:
To Shape Us

 ## Hard Work

Athletic coaches like to use the phrase "No pain, no gain." As a high school track star (Okay, maybe I wasn't that great, but I tried hard!), I heard coaches remind us again and again that the tough practice sessions would pay off when we began to compete. They were right. Oh, we didn't always win, but our hard work did produce obvious benefits.

I learned a lot about myself during those years. And now I'm learning even more as I discipline myself to jog daily. Many days I would just as soon forget it. I don't want to have to feel the pain of stretching exercises. I would rather not push my body's "radiator system" to the extreme. I would just as soon not have to battle fatigue as I go up the hills. So why do I do it? The gain is worth the pain. My blood pressure and pulse rate are kept low, my middle isn't expanding, and I feel more alert and healthy.

Exercise may have obvious benefits, but what about pain that we don't choose? What about illness, disease, accidents, and emotional agony? What kind of gain can come from those? Is the gain really worth the pain?

 # Fellow Sufferers

Let's consider what a fellow-sufferer had to say in Romans 5:3–4. The apostle Paul wrote, "We also glory in tribulations, knowing that tribulation produces perseverance; and perseverance, character; and character, hope."

Paul introduced his statement about the benefits of suffering by saying "we also glory in tribulations." How could he say that we should rejoice or be happy that we are having to endure some painful tragedy? He certainly was not telling us to celebrate our troubles; rather, he was telling us to rejoice about what God can and will do for us and for His glory through our trials. Paul's statement encourages us to celebrate the end product, not the painful process itself. He did not mean we are to get some sort of morbid joy out of death, cancer, deformity, financial reversals, a broken relationship, or a tragic accident. All these things are awful—a dark reminder that we live in a world that has been corrupted by the curse of sin's effects.

The apostle James also wrote about how we should rejoice in the end result of our troubles. He said, "My brethren, count it all joy when you fall into various trials, knowing that the testing of your faith produces patience. But let patience have its perfect work, that you may be perfect and complete, lacking nothing" (James 1:2–4).

As we combine the truths of these two passages, we can see how the good and praiseworthy products of suffering are patient perseverance, maturity of character, and hope. God can use the hardships of life to shape us to be more mature in the faith, more godly, more Christlike.

When we trust Christ as our Savior, the Lord does not suddenly zap us so that we become perfect people. What He does is remove sin's penalty and set us on the road that leads to heaven. Life then becomes a time of character development as we learn more about God and how we are to please Him. Suffering has a way of dramatically forcing us to deal with the deeper issues of life. By doing so, we grow stronger and gain maturity.

My grandfather, Dr. M. R. De Haan, spoke about the shaping process of our lives in his book *Broken Things*. He wrote:

> *The greatest sermons I have ever heard were not preached from pulpits but from sickbeds. The greatest, deepest truths of God's Word have often been revealed not by those who preached as a result of their seminary preparation and education, but by those humble souls who have gone through the seminary of affliction and have learned experientially the deep things of the ways of God.*
>
> *The most cheerful people I have met, with few exceptions, have been those who had the least sunshine and the most pain and suffering in their lives. The most grateful people I have met were not those who traveled a pathway of roses all their lives through, but those who were confined, because of circumstances, to their homes, often to their beds, and had learned to depend upon God as only such Christians know how to do. The gripers are usually, I have observed, those who enjoy excellent health. The complainers are those who have the least to complain about, and those dear saints of God who have refreshed my heart again and again as they preached from sickbed-pulpits have been the men and women who have been the most cheerful and the most grateful for the blessings of almighty God (pp. 43–44).*

How have you responded to the difficulties of life? Have you become bitter or better? Have you grown in your faith or turned away from God? Have you become more Christlike in your character? Have you let it shape you and conform you to the image of God's Son?

Together for Good?

Perhaps the most quoted part of the Bible during a time of pain and suffering is Romans 8:28. It reads, "We know that all things work together for good to those who love God, to those who are the called according to His purpose." This verse has often been misunderstood and perhaps misused, but its truth can bring a great deal of comfort.

The context of Romans 8 emphasizes what God is doing for us. The indwelling Holy Spirit gives us spiritual life (v. 9), reassures us that we are children of God (v. 16), and helps us with our prayers during our times of weakness (vv. 26–27). Romans 8 also puts our sufferings in the bigger picture of what God is doing—that God is working out His plan of redemption (vv. 18–26). Verses 28 through 39 reassure us of God's love for us, that no one or no thing could ever keep God from accomplishing what He wants to do, and that nothing could ever separate us from His love.

Properly viewed in the context of Romans 8, then, verse 28 powerfully reassures us that God is working on behalf of all who have trusted His Son as Savior. The verse does not promise that we will understand all the events of life or that after a time of testing we will be blessed with good things in this life. But it does reassure us that God is working out His good plan through our lives. He is shaping us and our circumstances to bring glory to himself.

Author Ron Lee Davis writes in his book *Becoming a Whole Person in a Broken World,* "The good news is not that God will make our circumstances come out the way we like, but that God can weave even our disappointments and disasters into His eternal plan. The evil that happens to us can be transformed into

God's good. Romans 8:28 is God's guarantee that if we love God, our lives can be used to achieve His purposes and further His kingdom" (p. 122).

"But," you may ask, "how can God be in control when life seems so out of control? How can He be working things together for His glory and our ultimate good?" In his book *Why Us?* Warren Wiersbe states that God "proves His sovereignty, not by intervening constantly and preventing these events, but by ruling and overruling them so that even tragedies end up accomplishing His ultimate purposes" (p. 136).

As the sovereign Lord of the universe, God is using all of life to develop our maturity and Christlikeness, and to further His eternal plan. In order to accomplish those purposes, however, God wants to use us to help others, and He wants other people to help us. That's what the next section is all about.

5 Suffering: To Shape Us

STUDY GUIDE
read pages 37–41

To see how pain and suffering can be an instrument to form us into the image of Christ.

MEMORY VERSE
James 1:2—
"My brethren, count it all joy when you fall into various trials."

Warming Up

Have you, like Dr. M. R. De Haan (p. 39), known sufferers who experienced great joy and peace? Have you also known people with great physical and material well-being who constantly complained? Where do you fit on that scale? _____

Thinking Through

1. In the analogy between athletic training and suffering (pp. 37–38), we see the "no pain, no gain" philosophy fully portrayed. Does this philosophy work equally well in the realms of illness, natural disasters, accidents, failures, and betrayals? Why or why not? _____

2. On page 39, Kurt says, "When we trust Christ as our Savior, the Lord does not suddenly zap us so that we become perfect people." Why not? Why is God's strategy of growth more significant than "instant perfection"? _____

3. Think about Warren Wiersbe's comment, on page 41, that God "proves His sovereignty, not by intervening constantly and preventing these events, but by ruling and overruling them so that even tragedies end up accomplishing His ultimate purposes." Can you validate that statement by your own observation of tragic events? By the record of tragedies in the Bible? _____

Going Further

Refer

Compare Romans 8:28 with Genesis 50:20, Ephesians 5:20, and 1 Thessalonians 5:18. What are the common principles found in these Scriptures? What comfort or assurance do they offer you? _____

1. "All things" is an all-encompassing phrase. Why is it more important that all things would work together for good than that all things would actually be good?

_____

_____

_____

_____

2. Using the context (vv. 26–28), explain how Paul described the Holy Spirit's role in this process of building our lives through "all things." Also, how does verse 28 relate to what God has done and is doing for us as described in Romans 8:16–39?

_____

_____

_____

_____

_____

3. Paul also used the phrase "all things" in verse 32. Is there a connection to the "all things" of verse 28? If so, what is it? How does Christ's suffering on our behalf assure God's ultimate goal (which is seen in verse 29)?

_____

_____

_____

_____

26 Likewise the Sprit also helps in our weaknesses. For we do not know what we should pray for as we ought, but the Spirit Himself makes intercession for us with groanings which cannot be uttered. 27 Now He who searches the hearts knows what the mind of the Spirit is, because He makes intercession for the saints according to the will of God. 28 And we know that all things work together for good to those who love God, to those who are the called according to His purpose. 29 For whom He foreknew, He also predestined to be conformed to the image of His Son, that He might be the firstborn among many brethren.

32 He who did not spare His own Son, but delivered Him up for us all, how shall He not with Him also freely give us all things?

Prayer Time ▶

Use the *Our Daily Bread* article on the next page as a guide for a devotional and meditation time relating to suffering.

Reflect

How have you responded to the difficulties of life? Have you become bitter or better? Have you grown in your faith or turned away from God? Have you become more Christlike in your character? Have you let your trials shape you and conform you to the image of God's Son? _____

_____

_____

Looking Up

Shortly before Scottish missionary John G. Paton died, a friend said to him, "I am sorry to see you lying on your back." Smiling, Paton asked, "Do you know why God puts us on our backs?" After his friend answered no, the missionary replied, "In order that we may look upward."

Another Christian who viewed suffering from the right perspective was songwriter Eugene Clark. Afflicted with severe rheumatoid arthritis and glaucoma, Clark spent the last 10 years of his life bedridden. Yet he continued composing songs and writing articles to the glory of God—enriching the lives of thousands through his ministry. Though down physically, he learned to keep looking up.

Sunny skies, worry-free days, and calm nights are not always the best environment for developing spiritual stamina. It is often in the hour of affliction that we draw close to our loving heavenly Father.

Perhaps you are undergoing some type of suffering right now. Rather than questioning God's providence, thank Him for His grace, lean on His strong arm, and look up into His face of love. You too can learn the valuable lesson learned by the writer of Psalm 119, John Paton, and Eugene Clark: Being down teaches us to look up.

—*Paul Van Gorder*

PSALM 119:71—
It is good for me that I have been afflicted, that I may learn Your statutes.

■ Read today's
Our Daily Bread at
www.rbc.org/odb

6

Suffering:
To Unite Us

Pain and suffering seem to have a special ability to show us how much we need each other. Our struggles remind us how fragile we really are. Even the weakness of others can bolster us when our own strength is sapped.

This truth becomes very real to me each time I meet with a small group of church friends for prayer and fellowship. During those regular times together, we have shared one another's burdens for a sick child, the loss of a job, workplace tensions, a rebellious child, a miscarriage, hostility among family members, depression, everyday stresses, an unsaved family member, tough decisions, neighborhood crime, battles with sin, and much more. Many times at the end of those meetings I have praised the Lord for the encouragement we have given to one another. We have been drawn closer and we have been strengthened as we have faced the struggles of life together.

These kinds of personal experiences in light of Scripture remind me of two key truths:

1. Suffering helps us to see our need of other believers.

2. Suffering helps us to meet the needs of others as we allow Christ to live through us.

Let's take a look at each of these ways God uses pain and suffering for the purpose of uniting us with other believers in Christ.

Need Others

In describing the unity of all believers in Christ, the apostle Paul used the analogy of a human body (1 Corinthians 12). He said that we need one another to function properly. Paul described the situation this way: "If one member suffers, all the members suffer with it; or if one member is honored, all the members rejoice with it. Now you are the body of Christ, and members individually" (vv. 26–27).

In his letter to the Ephesians, Paul spoke of Christ, "from whom the whole body, joined and knit together by what every joint supplies, according to the effective working by which every part does its share, causes growth of the body for the edifying of itself in love" (Ephesians 4:16).

When we begin to recognize what other believers have to offer us, then we will realize how much can be gained by reaching out for their help when we are going through a time of struggle. When troubles seem to knock out our strength, we can lean on other believers to help us find new strength in the Lord's power.

Meet Others' Needs

In 2 Corinthians 1, the apostle Paul wrote, "Blessed be the God and Father of our Lord Jesus Christ, the Father of mercies and God of all comfort, who comforts us in all our tribulation, that we may be able to comfort those who are in any trouble, with the comfort with which we ourselves are comforted by God" (vv. 3–4). As we saw in the previous section, we need one another because we have something valuable to offer.

We have spiritual insights and wisdom that we have learned as we have undergone trials of all sorts. We know the value of the personal presence of a loving person. When we experience the comfort of God during a troubling situation, we then have an ability to identify with those people who undergo similar situations.

While preparing to write this booklet, I read about the experiences of people who have suffered greatly, and I spoke with others who were familiar with pain. I searched to find out who helped them most in their time of trouble. The answer again and again has been this: another person who had undergone a similar experience. That person can empathize more fully, and his or her comments reflect understanding that comes by experience. To someone who is burdened down, it often sounds shallow and patronizing to hear another say,

When we begin to recognize what other believers have to offer us, then we will realize how much can be gained by reaching out for their help when we are going through a time of struggle.

"I understand what you are going through," unless that person has gone through a similar situation.

Even though the best comforters are those who have undergone similar situations and have grown spiritually stronger through them, that does not mean that the rest of us are off the hook. All of us have a responsibility to do all we can to empathize, to try to understand, to try to comfort. Galatians 6:2 tells us, "Bear one another's burdens, and so fulfill the law of Christ." And Romans 12:15 states, "Rejoice with those who rejoice, and weep with those who weep."

Dr. Paul Brand, an expert on the disease of leprosy, wrote, "When suffering strikes, those of us standing close by are flattened by the shock. We fight back the lumps in our throats, march resolutely to the hospital for visits, mumble a few cheerful words, perhaps look up articles on what to say to the grieving.

"But when I ask patients and their families, 'Who helped you in your suffering?' I hear a strange, imprecise answer. The person described rarely has smooth answers and a winsome, effervescent personality. It is someone quiet, understanding, who listens more than talks, who does not judge or even offer much advice. 'A sense of presence.' 'Someone there when I needed him.' A hand

● FOCAL POINT: Comfort

From the practical example of Paul, we can see that the help and consolation of the Holy Spirit often comes through brothers and sisters in Christ. They come alongside us and become the comfort vehicle that the Spirit of God uses. The Scriptures bear this out over and over as we are called on to comfort and encourage one another. In this respect, the role of comforter is carried out through every child of God who comes alongside a hurting person.

—Where Can We Find Comfort?

■ FOCAL POINT: Love

In short, there is no magic cure for a person in pain. Mainly, such a person needs love, for love instinctively detects what is needed.

— Philip Yancey

to hold, an understanding, bewildered hug. A shared lump in the throat" (*Fearfully And Wonderfully Made*, pp. 203–204).

It's clear—God made us to be dependent on one another. We have much to offer those in pain, and others have much to offer us as we endure troubles. As we develop that unity, we will experience greater comfort when we recognize that God uses suffering to alert us to the problems of sin, He uses difficulty to direct us to Him, and He can even use problems to make us more like Christ.

Suffering: To Unite Us

6

STUDY GUIDE
read pages 45–49

MEMORY VERSE
Galatians 6:2—
"Bear one another's
burdens, and so fulfill
the law of Christ."

To explore ways suffering can pull us together as a body of Christ and as fellow humans.

Warming Up

If you had to call someone at 3:00 a.m. to share your troubles, who would that be? Why?

Thinking Through

1. The biblical analogy of a human body illustrates the interrelatedness of believers (see p. 46). How does that metaphor display for us the way we should relate to one another as Christians?

2. Why is it dangerous to tell people that you know how they feel when you have not shared their experience? What are alternative ways you can offer comfort and support when you do not understand the specifics of a person's suffering?

3. Respond to the quote from Dr. Paul Brand on pages 48–49. How can this kind of support and concern fulfill the biblical command to "bear one another's burdens, and so fulfill the law of Christ" (Galatians 6:2)?

Going Further

Refer

The Gospels are filled with times when Christ displayed the comfort and mercy of God in His ministry. Identify at least two such incidents for each of these areas of suffering—physical suffering, emotional suffering, spiritual suffering, family suffering.

1. In verse 3, what three descriptions of God did Paul praise Him for? Why is each one important in your life as a child of God? How can these truths about God help us when we suffer and help us help others in their suffering?

3 Blessed be the God and Father of our Lord Jesus Christ, the Father of mercies and God of all comfort, 4 who comforts us in all our tribulation, that we may be able to comfort those who are in any trouble, with the comfort with which we ourselves are comforted by God. 5 For as the sufferings of Christ abound in us, so our consolation also abounds through Christ. 6 Now if we are afflicted, it is for your consolation and salvation, which is effective for enduring the same sufferings which we also suffer. Or if we are comforted, it is for your consolation and salvation. 7 And our hope for you is steadfast, because we know that as you are partakers of the sufferings, so also you will partake of the consolation.

2. According to verse 4, what is the reason God "comforts us in all our tribulation"? What, then, is our responsibility once we have been comforted by God?

3. What does verse 7, when viewed in light of Romans 12:15, say about the ministry of the body of Christ?

Prayer Time ▷

Use the Our Daily Bread article on the next page as a guide for a devotional and meditation time relating to suffering.

Reflect

Reflect on an occasion when God used someone to encourage you when you were on the verge of throwing in the towel. What did that person do that was helpful? Identify two people you know to be suffering right now. In what specific ways can you share God's comfort with them this week?

God Cares

In 1929, J. C. Penney learned a vital lesson about God's care. He was critically ill and had gone to the Kellogg Sanitarium in Battle Creek, Michigan, for treatment. One night, while in deep despair, he wrote farewell letters to his wife and son, telling them he did not expect to see the dawn.

But he survived the night, and the next day he had an experience that changed is life. He testified, "When I awoke the next morning, I was surprised to find that I was still alive. Going downstairs, I heard singing in a little chapel. They were singing 'God Will Take Care of You.' Going into the chapel, I listened with a weary heart to the singing, the reading of the Scripture lesson, and the prayer. Suddenly—something happened . . . . I felt as if I had been instantly lifted out of the darkness of a dungeon into warm, brilliant sunlight. I felt as if had been transported from hell to paradise. I felt the power of God as I never had felt it before; I realized that God with His love was there to help me."

Just as God promised Israel His help in Isaiah 41, He still provides our strength today. When a person realizes he is the special object of God's love, as J. C. Penney did, a deep peace settles into his life. This realization often comes in a time of anxiety or suffering. And when God's care becomes real to us, life never seems quite as distressing again. Yes, God cares!

—Dave Egner

ISAIAH 41:10—

Fear not, for I am with you; be not dismayed, for I am your God.

■ Read today's *Our Daily Bread* at **www.rbc.org/odb**

7

Final Thoughts:
How Can You Help?

Right now you may be overwhelmed by pain. The thought of trying to help someone else may seem impossible. At some point along the way, though, as you receive God's comfort, you will be ready to give comfort (2 Corinthians 1). In fact, reaching out to help others may be an important part of the process of your own emotional healing.

Or maybe you have read this booklet with the hope that you will be better able to help a hurting friend or loved one. The suggestions in this section are designed for you as well.

 ## Risky Business

Helping others is risky. Our help may not always be welcomed. We may sometimes say the wrong things. But try to help we must. Jesus' parable of the

Good Samaritan (Luke 10:25–37) reminds us that we are responsible to help the hurting people we encounter. Here are some suggestions:

- Don't wait for someone else to act first.
- Be physically present with them if possible and touch their hand or give an appropriate hug.
- Focus on their needs and not on your own discomfort with not having adequate answers.
- Allow them to express their feelings. Don't condemn their emotions.
- Learn about their problem.
- Don't pretend that you never struggle.
- Keep your words brief.
- Avoid saying, "You shouldn't feel that way," or, "You know what you should do."
- Assure them of your prayers.
- Pray! Ask God to help you and them.
- Keep in touch.
- Help them dispel false guilt by assuring them that suffering and sin are not inseparable twins.
- Help them find forgiveness in Christ if they are suffering due to sin, or if they become aware of some sin as they reflect on their lives.
- Encourage them to recall God's faithfulness in times past.
- Focus on Christ's example and help.
- Remind them that God loves us and cares for us and that He is in control.
- Encourage them to take one day at a time.
- Encourage them to reach out for the help they need (friends, family, pastor).
- Help them to realize that coping with troubles takes time.
- Remind them of God's shepherding love (Psalm 23).

- Remind them of God's control over the universe, both the big and small events of life.
- Don't ignore their problem.
- Don't be artificial in trying to "cheer them up." Be genuine. Be the friend you were to them before trouble hit.
- Show them the love you would like other people to show you if you were in their situation.
- Be a good listener.
- Acknowledge how much they hurt.
- Give them time to heal. Don't rush the process.

 # Better Than Answers

We cry out for complete answers. God offers himself instead. And that's enough. If we know that we can trust Him, we don't need full explanations. It's enough to know that our pain and suffering are not meaningless. It's enough to know that God still rules the universe and that He really does care about us as individuals.

The greatest evidence of God's concern for us can be found by looking at Jesus Christ. God loved our suffering world so much that He sent His Son to agonize and die for us, to free us from being sentenced to eternal sorrow (John 3:16–18). Because of Jesus, we can avoid the worst of all pain, the pain of separation from God—forever. And because of Christ, we can endure even the worst of tragedies now because of the strength He puts within us and the hope He sets before us.

The first step in coping realistically with the problem of suffering is to recognize its roots in the universal problem of sin. Have you recognized how much Jesus suffered on the cross for you to free you from the penalty of sin? Put your trust in Him. Receive His free gift of forgiveness. Only in Him will you find a lasting solution to the problem of pain in your life and in the world.

● LEADER'S and USER'S GUIDE

Overview of Lessons

Pulpit Sermon Series (for pastors and church leaders)

Although the Discovery Series Bible Study is primarily for personal and group study, pastors may want to use this material as the foundation for a series of messages on this important issue. The suggested topics and their corresponding texts from the Overview of Lessons above can be used as an outline for a sermon series.

DSBS User's Guide (for individuals and small groups)

Individuals—Personal Study

• Read the designated pages of the book.

• Carefully consider the study questions, and write out answers for each.

Small Groups—Bible-Study Discussion

• To maximize the value of the time spent together, each member should do the lesson work prior to the group meeting.

• Recommended discussion time: 45 minutes.

• Engage the group in a discussion of the questions—seeking full participation from each member.

Note To The Reader

The publisher invites you to share your reponse
to the message of this book by writing
Discovery House Publishers, P.O. Box 3566,
Grand Rapids, MI 49501, USA. For information
about other Discovery House books, music,
videos, or DVDs, contact us at the same
address or call 1-800-653-8333. Find us on the
Internet at **http://www.dhp.org/** or send e-mail
to **books@dhp.org**.